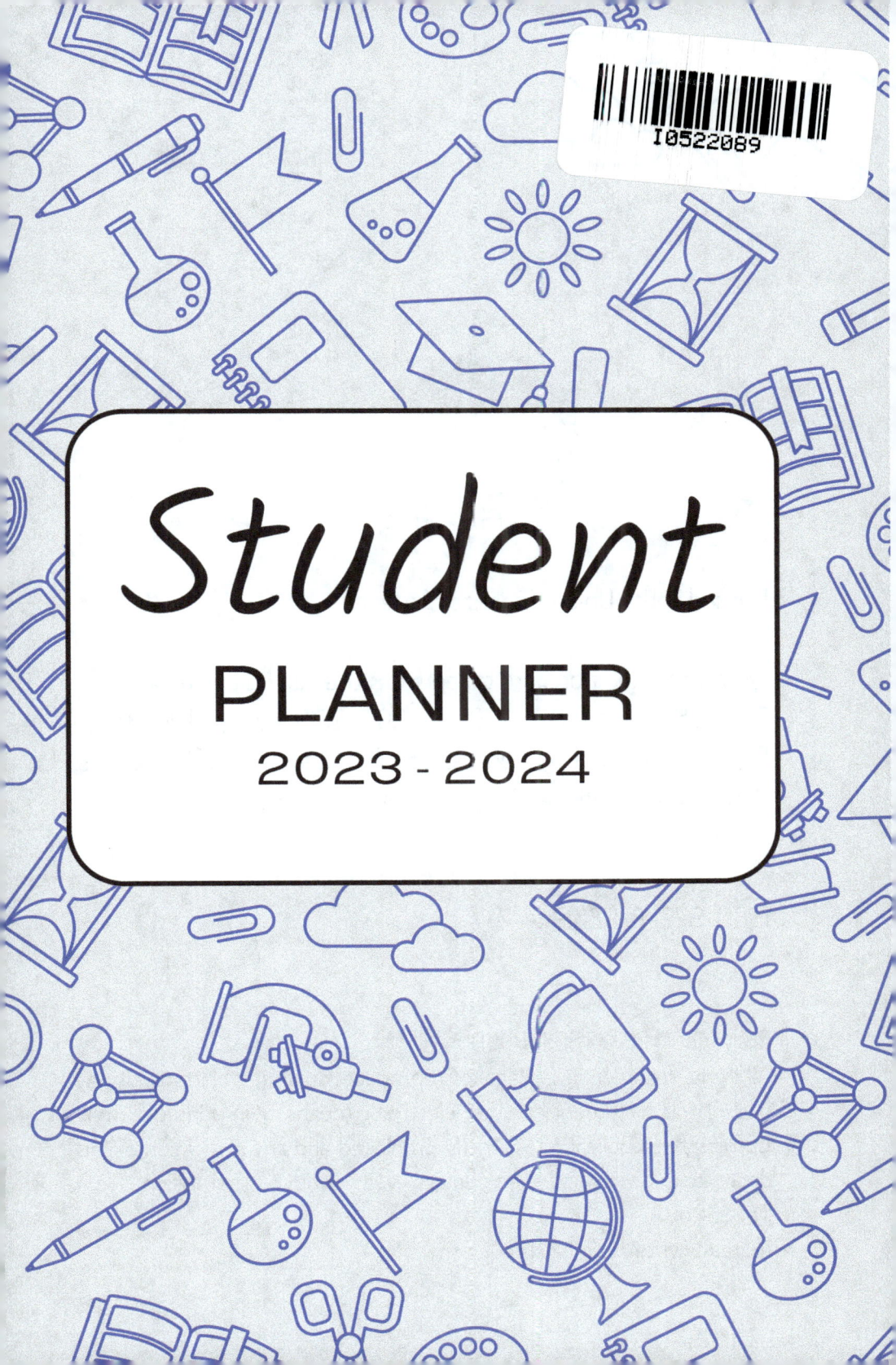

Student
PLANNER
2023 - 2024

ISBN: 979-8-9881944-7-7

PERSONAL INFORMATION

Full name: _____

Address: _____

City/Town: _____

State: _____

Postal code: _____

E-mail: _____

Telephone: _____

School: _____

School address: _____

School telephone: _____

Emergency contact: _____

Blood type: _____

Alergies: _____

Diseases: _____

> Seek the Kingdom of God above all else, and live righteously, and He will give you everything you need.
>
> *Matthew 6:33*

2023

JANUARY 23

S	M	T	W	T	F	S
1	2	3	4	5	6	7
8	9	10	11	12	13	14
15	16	17	18	19	20	21
22	23	24	25	26	27	28
29	30	31				

FEBRUARY 23

S	M	T	W	T	F	S
			1	2	3	4
5	6	7	8	9	10	11
12	13	14	15	16	17	18
19	20	21	22	23	24	25
26	27	28				

MARCH 23

S	M	T	W	T	F	S
			1	2	3	4
5	6	7	8	9	10	11
12	13	14	15	16	17	18
19	20	21	22	23	24	25
26	27	28	29	30	31	

APRIL 23

S	M	T	W	T	F	S
						1
2	3	4	5	6	7	8
9	10	11	12	13	14	15
16	17	18	19	20	21	22
23	24	25	26	27	28	29
30						

MAY 23

S	M	T	W	T	F	S
	1	2	3	4	5	6
7	8	9	10	11	12	13
14	15	16	17	18	19	20
21	22	23	24	25	26	27
28	29	30	31			

JUNE 23

S	M	T	W	T	F	S
				1	2	3
4	5	6	7	8	9	10
11	12	13	14	15	16	17
18	19	20	21	22	23	24
25	26	27	28	29	30	

JULY 23

S	M	T	W	T	F	S
						1
2	3	4	5	6	7	8
9	10	11	12	13	14	15
16	17	18	19	20	21	22
23	24	25	26	27	28	29
30	31					

AUGUST 23

S	M	T	W	T	F	S
		1	2	3	4	5
6	7	8	9	10	11	12
13	14	15	16	17	18	19
20	21	22	23	24	25	26
27	28	29	30	31		

SEPTEMBER 23

S	M	T	W	T	F	S
					1	2
3	4	5	6	7	8	9
10	11	12	13	14	15	16
17	18	19	20	21	22	23
24	25	26	27	28	29	30

OCTOBER 23

S	M	T	W	T	F	S
1	2	3	4	5	6	7
8	9	10	11	12	13	14
15	16	17	18	19	20	21
22	23	24	25	26	27	28
29	30	31				

NOVEMBER 23

S	M	T	W	T	F	S
			1	2	3	4
5	6	7	8	9	10	11
12	13	14	15	16	17	18
19	20	21	22	23	24	25
26	27	28	29	30		

DECEMBER 23

S	M	T	W	T	F	S
					1	2
3	4	5	6	7	8	9
10	11	12	13	14	15	16
17	18	19	20	21	22	23
24	25	26	27	28	29	30
31						

2024

January

S	M	T	W	T	F	S
	1	2	3	4	5	6
7	8	9	10	11	12	13
14	15	16	17	18	19	20
21	22	23	24	25	26	27
28	29	30	31			

February

S	M	T	W	T	F	S
				1	2	3
4	5	6	7	8	9	10
11	12	13	14	15	16	17
18	19	20	21	22	23	24
25	26	27	28	29		

March

S	M	T	W	T	F	S
					1	2
3	4	5	6	7	8	9
10	11	12	13	14	15	16
17	18	19	20	21	22	23
24	25	26	27	28	29	30
31						

April

S	M	T	W	T	F	S
	1	2	3	4	5	6
7	8	9	10	11	12	13
14	15	16	17	18	19	20
21	22	23	24	25	26	27
28	29	30				

May

S	M	T	W	T	F	S
			1	2	3	4
5	6	7	8	9	10	11
12	13	14	15	16	17	18
19	20	21	22	23	24	25
26	27	28	29	30	31	

June

S	M	T	W	T	F	S
						1
2	3	4	5	6	7	8
9	10	11	12	13	14	15
16	17	18	19	20	21	22
23	24	25	26	27	28	29
30						

July

S	M	T	W	T	F	S
	1	2	3	4	5	6
7	8	9	10	11	12	13
14	15	16	17	18	19	20
21	22	23	24	25	26	27
28	29	30	31			

August

S	M	T	W	T	F	S
				1	2	3
4	5	6	7	8	9	10
11	12	13	14	15	16	17
18	19	20	21	22	23	24
25	26	27	28	29	30	31

September

S	M	T	W	T	F	S
1	2	3	4	5	6	7
8	9	10	11	12	13	14
15	16	17	18	19	20	21
22	23	24	25	26	27	28
29	30					

October

S	M	T	W	T	F	S
		1	2	3	4	5
6	7	8	9	10	11	12
13	14	15	16	17	18	19
20	21	22	23	24	25	26
27	28	29	30	31		

November

S	M	T	W	T	F	S
					1	2
3	4	5	6	7	8	9
10	11	12	13	14	15	16
17	18	19	20	21	22	23
24	25	26	27	28	29	30

December

S	M	T	W	T	F	S
1	2	3	4	5	6	7
8	9	10	11	12	13	14
15	16	17	18	19	20	21
22	23	24	25	26	27	28
29	30	31				

Identifying
EMOTIONS

 funny	 happy	 sad	 disappointed	 exhausted
 silly	 shocked	 sneaky	 disgusted	 confused
 unimpressed	 loving	 playful	 ecstatic	 unenthused
 cheerful	 content	 relieved	 tired	 desperate
 embarrassed	 adoring	 neutral	 elated	 worried

"How to Study Effectively"

Make a Study Plan
When making a study schedule, look at your planner and think about what needs to be accomplished.

Steer Clear of Distrations
Be aware of what distracts you in class and know how to steer clear of these distractions.

Get Organized
Carry a homework planner at all times like entering homework, projects, tests and assignments, etc.

Start Studying More Effectively
Get more out of your study sessions with a complete study toolkit including note taking template, tips, ect.

Designate a Study Area
The best study spot is one that is quiet, well-it, and in a low-traffic area.

Simplify Study Notes
Make studying less overwhelming by condensing notes from class.

MULTIPLICATION

1
1 x 0 = 0
1 x 1 = 1
1 x 2 = 2
1 x 3 = 3
1 x 4 = 4
1 x 5 = 5
1 x 6 = 6
1 x 7 = 7
1 x 8 = 8
1 x 9 = 9
1 x 10 = 10
1 x 11 = 11
1 x 12 = 12

2
2 x 0 = 0
2 x 1 = 2
2 x 2 = 4
2 x 3 = 6
2 x 4 = 8
2 x 5 = 10
2 x 6 = 12
2 x 7 = 14
2 x 8 = 16
2 x 9 = 18
2 x 10 = 20
2 x 11 = 22
2 x 12 = 24

3
3 x 0 = 0
3 x 1 = 3
3 x 2 = 6
3 x 3 = 9
3 x 4 = 12
3 x 5 = 15
3 x 6 = 18
3 x 7 = 21
3 x 8 = 24
3 x 9 = 27
3 x 10 = 30
3 x 11 = 33
3 x 12 = 36

4
4 x 0 = 0
4 x 1 = 4
4 x 2 = 8
4 x 3 = 12
4 x 4 = 16
4 x 5 = 20
4 x 6 = 24
4 x 7 = 28
4 x 8 = 32
4 x 9 = 36
4 x 10 = 40
4 x 11 = 44
4 x 12 = 48

5
5 x 0 = 0
5 x 1 = 5
5 x 2 = 10
5 x 3 = 15
5 x 4 = 20
5 x 5 = 25
5 x 6 = 30
5 x 7 = 35
5 x 8 = 40
5 x 9 = 45
5 x 10 = 50
5 x 11 = 55
5 x 12 = 60

6
6 x 0 = 0
6 x 1 = 6
6 x 2 = 12
6 x 3 = 18
6 x 4 = 24
6 x 5 = 30
6 x 6 = 36
6 x 7 = 42
6 x 8 = 48
6 x 9 = 54
6 x 10 = 60
6 x 11 = 66
6 x 12 = 72

7
7 x 0 = 0
7 x 1 = 7
7 x 2 = 14
7 x 3 = 21
7 x 4 = 28
7 x 5 = 35
7 x 6 = 42
7 x 7 = 49
7 x 8 = 56
7 x 9 = 63
7 x 10 = 70
7 x 11 = 77
7 x 12 = 84

8
8 x 0 = 0
8 x 1 = 8
8 x 2 = 16
8 x 3 = 24
8 x 4 = 32
8 x 5 = 40
8 x 6 = 48
8 x 7 = 56
8 x 8 = 64
8 x 9 = 72
8 x 10 = 80
8 x 11 = 88
8 x 12 = 96

9
9 x 0 = 0
9 x 1 = 9
9 x 2 = 18
9 x 3 = 27
9 x 4 = 36
9 x 5 = 45
9 x 6 = 54
9 x 7 = 63
9 x 8 = 72
9 x 9 = 81
9 x 10 = 90
9 x 11 = 99
9 x 12 = 108

10
10 x 0 = 0
10 x 1 = 10
10 x 2 = 20
10 x 3 = 30
10 x 4 = 40
10 x 5 = 50
10 x 6 = 60
10 x 7 = 70
10 x 8 = 80
10 x 9 = 90
10 x 10 = 100
10 x 11 = 110
10 x 12 = 120

11
11 x 0 = 0
11 x 1 = 11
11 x 2 = 22
11 x 3 = 33
11 x 4 = 44
11 x 5 = 55
11 x 6 = 66
11 x 7 = 77
11 x 8 = 88
11 x 9 = 99
11 x 10 = 110
11 x 11 = 121
11 x 12 = 132

12
12 x 0 = 0
12 x 1 = 12
12 x 2 = 24
12 x 3 = 36
12 x 4 = 48
12 x 5 = 60
12 x 6 = 72
12 x 7 = 84
12 x 8 = 96
12 x 9 = 108
12 x 10 = 120
12 x 11 = 132
12 x 12 = 144

MEASUREMENT CONVERSIONS

LENGTH

Customary Units

1 Foot = 12 Inches

1 Yard = 3 Feet

1 Mile = 5,280 Feet

Metric Units

1 Kilometer = 1,000 Meters

1 Meter = 100 centimeters

1 centimeter = 10 millimeters

CAPACITY

Customary Units

1 Gallon = 4 Quarts

1 Quart = 2 Pints

1 Pint = 2 Cups

1 Cup = 8 Fluid Ounces

Metric Units

1 liter = 10 Deciliters

1 liter = 1000 Millimeters

WEIGHT

Customary Units

1 Pound = 16 Ounces

1 Ton = 2,000 pounds

MASS

Metric Units

1 Kilogram = 1,000 Grams

1 Gram = 1,000 Milligrams

TIME

1 Minute = 60 Seconds

1 Hour = 60 Minutes

1 Day = 24 Hours

1 Week = 7 Days

1 Year = 12 Months

1 Year = 52 Weeks

1 Year = 365 Days

1 Leap Year = 366

Angles & Their Measures

Do you want to build something? Understanding and measuring angles is essential when working with space, whether you want to improve an existing project or start a new one!

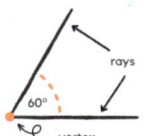

What are angles?

Formed when two rays or line segments meet at a common endpoint called **vertex**.

How to measure an angle using a protractor?

Step 1:

Place the protractor's center point at the angle's vertex.

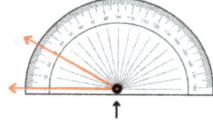

Step 2:

Align the protractor's bottom line with the bottom ray of the angle at the 0 mark.

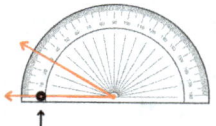

Step 3:

Find the angle measure by reading the number where the second ray intersects the protractor.

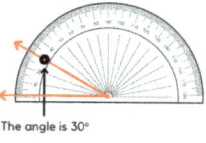

The angle is 30°

Mastering Angles with a Protractor

The angle is 50°.

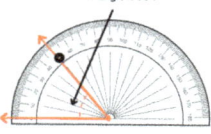

The angle is 130°.

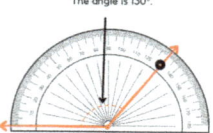

Exponent Rules

Exponent of Zero ✕

$$a^0 = 1$$

A base with an exponent of 0 is always equal to 1.

Exponent of One ✕

$$a^1 = a$$

Any number raised to an exponent of 1 is equal to itself.

Exponent of Product ✕

$$a^m \times a^n = a^{m+n}$$

When multiplying exponential terms with the same base, add the powers.

Exponent of Quotient ✕

$$\frac{a^m}{a^n} = a^{m-n}$$

When dividing exponential terms with the same base, subtract the powers.

Exponent of Power ✕

$$(a^m)^n = a^{mn}$$

When a power is raised to another power, multiply the exponents.

Exponent Negative ✕

$$a^{-n} = \frac{1}{a^n}$$

When a number is raised to a negative power, divide 1 by the base raised to the positive exponent.

AUTHOR'S PURPOSE

FOUND IN:
- NEWSPAPER/MAGAZINE ARTICLES
- AUTOBIOGRAPHIES
- NONFICTION BOOKS
- BIOGRAPHIES

FOUND IN:
- POETRY
- FICTION BOOKS
  - FANTASY STORIES

INFORM

When the author writes about a factual topic.

ENTERTAIN

When the author writes about funny, interesting or new topics to keep your attention.

READER'S PURPOSE:
- I LEARNED THAT...
- NOW, I KNOW...

READER'S PURPOSE:
- IT WAS FUNNY WHEN...
- MY FAVOURITE PART WAS...

PERSUADE

When the author writes about something with the intention of changing your opinion to theirs.

FOUND IN:
- NEWSPAPER/MAGAZINE ARTICLES
- ADVERTISEMENTS
- COMMERCIALS
- DEBATES

READER'S PURPOSE:
- I BELIEVE THAT...
- I CHANGE MY MIND ABOUT...

TYPES OF NOUNS

Proper Noun
Specific names for people, places or things.

A person's name. The name of a place. The name of a thing.

Common Noun
General names for people, places or things.

People: Mom   Place: Park   Thing: Toy

Concrete Noun
Things that you can see, touch, hear, smell, or taste.

Tree. Cat. Dog. Flower. Apple.

Abstract Noun
Ideas or feelings or qualities you cannot perceive with your senses.

Love. Happiness. Bravery. Friendship.

Collective Noun
Groups or collections of people or things.

Team. Family. Class.

Possesive Noun
Shows ownership or possession.

John's car. The dog's tail. The teacher's book.

Countable Noun
Things that can be counted.

Dollars. Classmates. Books.

Uncountable Noun
Things that cannot be counted.

Water. Sand. Knowledge.

Commit your actions to the Lord, and your plans will succeed.

Proverbs 16:3

SCHOOL YEAR OVERVIEW

JULY

AUGUST

SEPTEMBER

OCTOBER

NOVEMBER

DECEMBER

JANUARY

FEBRUARY

MARCH

APRIL

MAY

JUNE

CLASS/ACTIVITY SCHEDULE
SEMESTER 1

TIME	MONDAY	TUESDAY	WEDNESDAY	THURSDAY	FRIDAY
7 - 8 am					
8 - 9 am					
9 - 10 am					
10 - 11 am					
11 am - 12 pm					
12 - 1 pm					
1 - 2 pm					
2 - 3 pm					
3 - 4 pm					
4 - 5 pm					
5 - 6 pm					
6 - 7 pm					
7 - 9 pm					

CLASS/ACTIVITY SCHEDULE
SEMESTER 2

TIME	MONDAY	TUESDAY	WEDNESDAY	THURSDAY	FRIDAY
7 - 8 am					
8 - 9 am					
9 - 10 am					
10 - 11 am					
11 am - 12pm					
12 - 1 pm					
1 - 2 pm					
2 - 3 pm					
3 - 4 pm					
4 - 5 pm					
5 - 6 pm					
6 - 7 pm					
7 - 9 pm					

Work willingly at whatever you do, as though you were working for Lord rather than for people.
Colossians 3:23

August

SU	MC	TU	WE	TH	FR	SA
		1	2	3	4	5
6	7	8	9	10	11	12
13	14	15	16	17	18	19
20	21	22	23	24	25	26
27	28	29	30	31		

Notes:

_____
_____
_____
_____
_____
_____
_____
_____

Week Of: _____

Sunday

_____ _____
_____ _____
_____ _____
_____ _____
_____ _____

Monday

_____ _____
_____ _____
_____ _____
_____ _____
_____ _____

Tuesday

_____ _____
_____ _____
_____ _____
_____ _____

Wednesday

_____ _____
_____ _____
_____ _____
_____ _____

Positive Affirmation:_____
_____
_____

Thursday

_____ _____
_____ _____
_____ _____
_____ _____
_____ _____

Friday

_____ _____
_____ _____
_____ _____
_____ _____
_____ _____

Saturday

_____ _____
_____ _____
_____ _____
_____ _____
_____ _____

Notes

_____ _____
_____ _____
_____ _____
_____ _____
_____ _____

Week Of: _____

Sunday

_____   _____
_____   _____
_____   _____
_____   _____
_____   _____

Monday

_____   _____
_____   _____
_____   _____
_____   _____
_____   _____

Tuesday

_____   _____
_____   _____
_____   _____
_____   _____
_____   _____

Wednesday

_____   _____
_____   _____
_____   _____
_____   _____

Positive Affirmation:_____
_____
_____

Thursday

_____   _____
_____   _____
_____   _____
_____   _____
_____   _____

Friday

_____   _____
_____   _____
_____   _____
_____   _____
_____   _____

Saturday

_____   _____
_____   _____
_____   _____
_____   _____
_____   _____

Notes

_____   _____
_____   _____
_____   _____
_____   _____
_____   _____

Week Of: _____

Sunday

Monday

Tuesday

Wednesday

Positive Affirmation:_____
_____
_____

Thursday

_____ _____
_____ _____
_____ _____
_____ _____
_____ _____

Friday

_____ _____
_____ _____
_____ _____
_____ _____
_____ _____

Saturday

_____ _____
_____ _____
_____ _____
_____ _____

Notes

_____ _____
_____ _____
_____ _____
_____ _____

Week Of: _____

Sunday

_____   _____
_____   _____
_____   _____
_____   _____
_____   _____
_____

Monday

_____   _____
_____   _____
_____   _____
_____   _____
_____   _____
_____

Tuesday

_____   _____
_____   _____
_____   _____
_____   _____
_____   _____
_____

Wednesday

_____   _____
_____   _____
_____   _____
_____   _____
_____

Positive Affirmation:_____
_____
_____

Thursday

_____   _____
_____   _____
_____   _____
_____   _____
_____   _____

Friday

_____   _____
_____   _____
_____   _____
_____   _____
_____   _____

Saturday

_____   _____
_____   _____
_____   _____
_____   _____
_____   _____

Notes

_____   _____
_____   _____
_____   _____
_____   _____
_____   _____

Trust in the Lord with all your heart; do not depend on your own understanding.

Proverbs 3:5

September

SU	MO	TU	WE	TH	FR	SA
					1	2
3	4	5	6	7	8	9
10	11	12	13	14	15	16
17	18	19	20	21	22	23
24	25	26	27	28	29	30

Notes:

_____
_____
_____
_____
_____
_____
_____
_____

Week Of: _____

Sunday

_____   _____
_____   _____
_____   _____
_____   _____
_____   _____

Monday

_____   _____
_____   _____
_____   _____
_____   _____
_____   _____

Tuesday

_____   _____
_____   _____
_____   _____
_____   _____
_____   _____

Wednesday

_____   _____
_____   _____
_____   _____
_____   _____
_____   _____

Positive Affirmation:_____
_____
_____

Thursday

_____   _____
_____   _____
_____   _____
_____   _____
_____   _____

Friday

_____   _____
_____   _____
_____   _____
_____   _____
_____   _____

Saturday

_____   _____
_____   _____
_____   _____
_____   _____

Notes

_____   _____
_____   _____
_____   _____
_____   _____

Week Of: _____

Sunday

_____   _____
_____   _____
_____   _____
_____   _____
_____

Monday

_____   _____
_____   _____
_____   _____
_____   _____
_____

Tuesday

_____   _____
_____   _____
_____   _____
_____   _____
_____

Wednesday

_____   _____
_____   _____
_____   _____
_____   _____
_____

Positive Affirmation:_____
_____
_____

Thursday

_____   _____
_____   _____
_____   _____
_____   _____
_____

Friday

_____   _____
_____   _____
_____   _____
_____   _____
_____

Saturday

_____   _____
_____   _____
_____   _____
_____

Notes

_____   _____
_____   _____
_____   _____
_____   _____

Week Of: _____

Sunday

_____ _____
_____ _____
_____ _____
_____ _____
_____ _____

Monday

_____ _____
_____ _____
_____ _____
_____ _____
_____ _____

Tuesday

_____ _____
_____ _____
_____ _____
_____ _____
_____ _____

Wednesday

_____ _____
_____ _____
_____ _____
_____ _____
_____ _____

Positive Affirmation:_____
_____
_____

Thursday

_____ _____
_____ _____
_____ _____
_____ _____
_____ _____

Friday

_____ _____
_____ _____
_____ _____
_____ _____
_____ _____

Saturday

_____ _____
_____ _____
_____ _____
_____ _____

Notes

_____ _____
_____ _____
_____ _____
_____ _____

Week Of: _____

Sunday

_____ _____
_____ _____
_____ _____
_____ _____
_____ _____

Monday

_____ _____
_____ _____
_____ _____
_____ _____
_____ _____

Tuesday

_____ _____
_____ _____
_____ _____
_____ _____
_____ _____

Wednesday

_____ _____
_____ _____
_____ _____
_____ _____
_____ _____

Positive Affirmation:_____
_____
_____

Thursday

Friday

Saturday

Notes

Never be lazy, but work hard and serve the Lord enthusiastically.

Romans 12:11

October

SU	MO	TU	WE	TH	FR	SA
1	2	3	4	5	6	7
8	9	10	11	12	13	14
15	16	17	18	19	20	21
22	23	24	25	26	27	28
29	30	31				

Notes:

_____
_____
_____
_____
_____
_____
_____

Week Of: _____

Sunday

_____   _____
_____   _____
_____   _____
_____   _____
_____   _____

Monday

_____   _____
_____   _____
_____   _____
_____   _____
_____   _____

Tuesday

_____   _____
_____   _____
_____   _____
_____   _____
_____   _____

Wednesday

_____   _____
_____   _____
_____   _____
_____   _____
_____   _____

Positive Affirmation:_____
_____
_____

Thursday

Friday

Saturday

Notes

Week Of: _____

Sunday

_____ _____
_____ _____
_____ _____
_____ _____
_____ _____

Monday

_____ _____
_____ _____
_____ _____
_____ _____
_____ _____

Tuesday

_____ _____
_____ _____
_____ _____
_____ _____
_____ _____

Wednesday

_____ _____
_____ _____
_____ _____
_____ _____

Positive Affirmation:_____
_____
_____

Thursday

_____   _____
_____   _____
_____   _____
_____   _____
_____

Friday

_____   _____
_____   _____
_____   _____
_____   _____
_____

Saturday

_____   _____
_____   _____
_____   _____
_____   _____
_____

Notes

_____   _____
_____   _____
_____   _____
_____   _____
_____

Week Of: _____

Sunday

_____   _____
_____   _____
_____   _____
_____   _____
_____   _____

Monday

_____   _____
_____   _____
_____   _____
_____   _____
_____   _____

Tuesday

_____   _____
_____   _____
_____   _____
_____   _____

Wednesday

_____   _____
_____   _____
_____   _____
_____

Positive Affirmation:_____
_____
_____

Thursday

Friday

Saturday

Notes

Week Of: _____

Sunday

_____ _____
_____ _____
_____ _____
_____ _____
_____ _____

Monday

_____ _____
_____ _____
_____ _____
_____ _____
_____ _____

Tuesday

_____ _____
_____ _____
_____ _____
_____ _____
_____ _____

Wednesday

_____ _____
_____ _____
_____ _____
_____ _____

Positive Affirmation:_____
_____
_____

Thursday

Friday

Saturday

Notes

Get the truth and never sell it; also get wisdom, discipline, and good judgment.

Proverbs 23:23

November

SU	MO	TU	WE	TH	FR	SA
			1	2	3	4
5	6	7	8	9	10	11
12	13	14	15	16	17	18
19	20	21	22	23	24	25
26	27	28	29	30		

Notes:

_____
_____
_____
_____
_____
_____
_____
_____

Week Of: _____

Sunday

_____ _____
_____ _____
_____ _____
_____ _____
_____ _____

Monday

_____ _____
_____ _____
_____ _____
_____ _____
_____ _____

Tuesday

_____ _____
_____ _____
_____ _____
_____ _____
_____ _____

Wednesday

_____ _____
_____ _____
_____ _____
_____ _____
_____ _____

Positive Affirmation:_____
_____
_____

Thursday

Friday

Saturday

Notes

Week Of: _____

Sunday

_____   _____
_____   _____
_____   _____
_____   _____
_____   _____

Monday

_____   _____
_____   _____
_____   _____
_____   _____
_____   _____

Tuesday

_____   _____
_____   _____
_____   _____
_____   _____
_____   _____

Wednesday

_____   _____
_____   _____
_____   _____
_____   _____
_____   _____

Positive Affirmation:_____

_____

_____

Thursday

Friday

Saturday

Notes

Week Of: _____

Sunday
_____   _____
_____   _____
_____   _____
_____   _____
_____   _____

Monday
_____   _____
_____   _____
_____   _____
_____   _____
_____   _____

Tuesday
_____   _____
_____   _____
_____   _____
_____   _____
_____   _____

Wednesday
_____   _____
_____   _____
_____   _____
_____   _____
_____   _____

Positive Affirmation:_____

_____

_____

Thursday

_____ _____

_____ _____

_____ _____

_____ _____

_____ _____

Friday

_____ _____

_____ _____

_____ _____

_____ _____

_____ _____

Saturday

_____ _____

_____ _____

_____ _____

_____ _____

_____ _____

Notes

_____ _____

_____ _____

_____ _____

_____ _____

Week Of: _____

Sunday

_____ _____
_____ _____
_____ _____
_____ _____
_____ _____

Monday

_____ _____
_____ _____
_____ _____
_____ _____
_____ _____

Tuesday

_____ _____
_____ _____
_____ _____
_____ _____
_____ _____

Wednesday

_____ _____
_____ _____
_____ _____
_____ _____
_____ _____

Positive Affirmation:_____
_____
_____

Thursday

Friday

Saturday

Notes

Think about what I am saying. The Lord will help you understand all these things.

2 Timothy 2:7

December

SU	MO	TU	WE	TH	FR	SA
					1	2
3	4	5	6	7	8	9
10	11	12	13	14	15	16
17	18	19	20	21	22	23
24	25	26	27	28	29	30
31						

Notes:

Week Of: _____

Sunday
_____ _____
_____ _____
_____ _____
_____ _____
_____ _____

Monday
_____ _____
_____ _____
_____ _____
_____ _____
_____ _____

Tuesday
_____ _____
_____ _____
_____ _____
_____ _____
_____ _____

Wednesday
_____ _____
_____ _____
_____ _____
_____ _____

Positive Affirmation:_____

_____

_____

Thursday

_____   _____
_____   _____
_____   _____
_____   _____
_____   _____

Friday

_____   _____
_____   _____
_____   _____
_____   _____
_____   _____

Saturday

_____   _____
_____   _____
_____   _____
_____   _____
_____   _____

Notes

_____   _____
_____   _____
_____   _____
_____   _____
_____   _____

Week Of: _____

Sunday

_____ _____
_____ _____
_____ _____
_____ _____
_____ _____

Monday

_____ _____
_____ _____
_____ _____
_____ _____
_____ _____

Tuesday

_____ _____
_____ _____
_____ _____
_____ _____
_____ _____

Wednesday

_____ _____
_____ _____
_____ _____
_____ _____
_____ _____

Positive Affirmation:_____
_____
_____

Thursday

_____   _____
_____   _____
_____   _____
_____   _____
_____   _____

Friday

_____   _____
_____   _____
_____   _____
_____   _____
_____   _____

Saturday

_____   _____
_____   _____
_____   _____
_____   _____
_____   _____

Notes

_____   _____
_____   _____
_____   _____
_____   _____

Week Of: _____

Sunday

_____ _____
_____ _____
_____ _____
_____ _____
_____

Monday

_____ _____
_____ _____
_____ _____
_____ _____
_____

Tuesday

_____ _____
_____ _____
_____ _____
_____ _____
_____

Wednesday

_____ _____
_____ _____
_____ _____
_____ _____
_____

Positive Affirmation:_____
_____
_____

Thursday

_____ _____
_____ _____
_____ _____
_____ _____
_____ _____

Friday

_____ _____
_____ _____
_____ _____
_____ _____
_____ _____

Saturday

_____ _____
_____ _____
_____ _____
_____ _____
_____ _____

Notes

_____ _____
_____ _____
_____ _____
_____ _____

Week Of: _____

Sunday
_____ _____
_____ _____
_____ _____
_____ _____
_____ _____

Monday
_____ _____
_____ _____
_____ _____
_____ _____
_____ _____

Tuesday
_____ _____
_____ _____
_____ _____
_____ _____
_____ _____

Wednesday
_____ _____
_____ _____
_____ _____
_____ _____

Positive Affirmation:_____
_____
_____

Thursday

_____ _____
_____ _____
_____ _____
_____ _____
_____

Friday

_____ _____
_____ _____
_____ _____
_____ _____
_____

Saturday

_____ _____
_____ _____
_____ _____
_____ _____
_____

Notes

_____ _____
_____ _____
_____ _____
_____ _____

Study this Book of Instruction continually. Meditate on it day and night so you will be sure to obey everything written in it. Only then will you prosper and succeed in all you do. *Joshua 1:8*

January

SU	MO	TU	WE	TH	FR	SA
	1	2	3	4	5	6
7	8	9	10	11	12	13
14	15	16	17	18	19	20
21	22	23	24	25	26	27
28	29	30	31			

Notes:

Week Of: _____

Sunday

_____ _____
_____ _____
_____ _____
_____ _____
_____ _____

Monday

_____ _____
_____ _____
_____ _____
_____ _____
_____ _____

Tuesday

_____ _____
_____ _____
_____ _____
_____ _____
_____ _____

Wednesday

_____ _____
_____ _____
_____ _____
_____ _____

Positive Affirmation:_____

_____

_____

Thursday

Friday

Saturday

Notes

Week Of: _____

Sunday

_____   _____
_____   _____
_____   _____
_____   _____
_____   _____

Monday

_____   _____
_____   _____
_____   _____
_____   _____
_____   _____

Tuesday

_____   _____
_____   _____
_____   _____
_____   _____
_____   _____

Wednesday

_____   _____
_____   _____
_____   _____
_____   _____
_____   _____

Positive Affirmation:_____
_____
_____

Thursday

Friday

Saturday

Notes

Week Of: _____

Sunday

_____ _____
_____ _____
_____ _____
_____ _____
_____ _____

Monday

_____ _____
_____ _____
_____ _____
_____ _____
_____ _____

Tuesday

_____ _____
_____ _____
_____ _____
_____ _____
_____ _____

Wednesday

_____ _____
_____ _____
_____ _____
_____ _____

Positive Affirmation:_____

_____

_____

Thursday

_____   _____
_____   _____
_____   _____
_____   _____
_____   _____

Friday

_____   _____
_____   _____
_____   _____
_____   _____
_____   _____

Saturday

_____   _____
_____   _____
_____   _____
_____   _____

Notes

_____   _____
_____   _____
_____   _____
_____   _____

Week Of: _____

Sunday

_____   _____
_____   _____
_____   _____
_____   _____
_____   _____

Monday

_____   _____
_____   _____
_____   _____
_____   _____
_____   _____

Tuesday

_____   _____
_____   _____
_____   _____
_____   _____
_____   _____

Wednesday

_____   _____
_____   _____
_____   _____
_____   _____
_____   _____

Positive Affirmation:_____
_____
_____

Thursday

Friday

Saturday

Notes

For I can do everything through Christ, who gives me strength.

Philippians 4:13

February

SU	MO	TU	WE	TH	FR	SA
				1	2	3
4	5	6	7	8	9	10
11	12	13	14	15	16	17
18	19	20	21	22	23	24
25	26	27	28	29		

Notes:

_____

_____

_____

_____

_____

_____

_____

Week Of: _____

Sunday

_____ _____
_____ _____
_____ _____
_____ _____
_____ _____

Monday

_____ _____
_____ _____
_____ _____
_____ _____
_____ _____

Tuesday

_____ _____
_____ _____
_____ _____
_____ _____
_____ _____

Wednesday

_____ _____
_____ _____
_____ _____
_____ _____

Positive Affirmation:_____
_____
_____

Thursday

Friday

Saturday

Notes

Week Of: _____

Sunday

_____ _____
_____ _____
_____ _____
_____ _____

Monday

_____ _____
_____ _____
_____ _____
_____ _____

Tuesday

_____ _____
_____ _____
_____ _____
_____ _____

Wednesday

_____ _____
_____ _____
_____ _____
_____ _____

Positive Affirmation:_____
_____
_____

Thursday

_____   _____
_____   _____
_____   _____
_____   _____
_____   _____

Friday

_____   _____
_____   _____
_____   _____
_____   _____
_____   _____

Saturday

_____   _____
_____   _____
_____   _____
_____   _____
_____   _____

Notes

_____   _____
_____   _____
_____   _____
_____   _____
_____   _____

Week Of: _____

Sunday

_____   _____
_____   _____
_____   _____
_____   _____
_____   _____

Monday

_____   _____
_____   _____
_____   _____
_____   _____
_____   _____

Tuesday

_____   _____
_____   _____
_____   _____
_____   _____
_____   _____

Wednesday

_____   _____
_____   _____
_____   _____
_____   _____

Positive Affirmation:_____
_____
_____

Thursday
_____   _____
_____   _____
_____   _____
_____   _____
_____   _____

Friday
_____   _____
_____   _____
_____   _____
_____   _____
_____   _____

Saturday
_____   _____
_____   _____
_____   _____
_____   _____

Notes
_____   _____
_____   _____
_____   _____
_____   _____

Week Of: _____

Sunday

_____ _____
_____ _____
_____ _____
_____ _____
_____ _____

Monday

_____ _____
_____ _____
_____ _____
_____ _____
_____ _____

Tuesday

_____ _____
_____ _____
_____ _____
_____ _____
_____ _____

Wednesday

_____ _____
_____ _____
_____ _____
_____ _____

Positive Affirmation:_____
_____
_____

Thursday

Friday

Saturday

Notes

But as for you, be strong and courageous, for your work will be rewarded.

2 Chronicles 15:7

March

SU	MO	TU	WE	TH	FR	SA
					1	2
3	4	5	6	7	8	9
10	11	12	13	14	15	16
17	18	19	20	21	22	23
24	25	26	27	28	29	30
31						

Notes:

Week Of: _____

Sunday
_____   _____
_____   _____
_____   _____
_____   _____
_____   _____

Monday
_____   _____
_____   _____
_____   _____
_____   _____
_____   _____

Tuesday
_____   _____
_____   _____
_____   _____
_____   _____
_____   _____

Wednesday
_____   _____
_____   _____
_____   _____
_____   _____
_____   _____

Positive Affirmation:_____

_____

_____

Thursday

_____   _____
_____   _____
_____   _____
_____   _____
_____   _____

Friday

_____   _____
_____   _____
_____   _____
_____   _____
_____   _____

Saturday

_____   _____
_____   _____
_____   _____
_____   _____

Notes

_____   _____
_____   _____
_____   _____
_____   _____

Week Of: _____

Sunday

_____ _____
_____ _____
_____ _____
_____ _____
_____ _____

Monday

_____ _____
_____ _____
_____ _____
_____ _____
_____ _____

Tuesday

_____ _____
_____ _____
_____ _____
_____ _____

Wednesday

_____ _____
_____ _____
_____ _____
_____ _____

Positive Affirmation:_____

_____

_____

Thursday

Friday

Saturday

Notes

Week Of: _____

Sunday

_____ _____
_____ _____
_____ _____
_____ _____
_____ _____

Monday

_____ _____
_____ _____
_____ _____
_____ _____
_____ _____

Tuesday

_____ _____
_____ _____
_____ _____
_____ _____
_____ _____

Wednesday

_____ _____
_____ _____
_____ _____
_____ _____
_____ _____

Positive Affirmation:_____
_____
_____

Thursday

Friday

Saturday

Notes

Week Of: _____

Sunday
_____ _____
_____ _____
_____ _____
_____ _____
_____ _____

Monday
_____ _____
_____ _____
_____ _____
_____ _____
_____ _____

Tuesday
_____ _____
_____ _____
_____ _____
_____ _____
_____ _____

Wednesday
_____ _____
_____ _____
_____ _____
_____ _____

Positive Affirmation:_____
_____
_____

Thursday

_____   _____
_____   _____
_____   _____
_____   _____
_____   _____

Friday

_____   _____
_____   _____
_____   _____
_____   _____
_____   _____

Saturday

_____   _____
_____   _____
_____   _____
_____   _____

Notes

_____   _____
_____   _____
_____   _____
_____   _____

And we know that God causes everything to work together for the good of those who love God and care called according to His purpose for them.
Romans 8:28

April

SU	MO	TU	WE	TH	FR	SA
	1	2	3	4	5	6
7	8	9	10	11	12	13
14	15	16	17	18	19	20
21	22	23	24	25	26	27
28	29	30				

Notes:

_____
_____
_____
_____
_____
_____
_____
_____

Week Of: _____

Sunday

_____   _____
_____   _____
_____   _____
_____   _____
_____   _____

Monday

_____   _____
_____   _____
_____   _____
_____   _____
_____   _____

Tuesday

_____   _____
_____   _____
_____   _____
_____   _____
_____   _____

Wednesday

_____   _____
_____   _____
_____   _____
_____   _____

Positive Affirmation:_____
_____
_____

Thursday

Friday

Saturday

Notes

Week Of: _____

Sunday

_____   _____
_____   _____
_____   _____
_____   _____
_____   _____

Monday

_____   _____
_____   _____
_____   _____
_____   _____
_____   _____

Tuesday

_____   _____
_____   _____
_____   _____
_____   _____
_____   _____

Wednesday

_____   _____
_____   _____
_____   _____
_____   _____
_____   _____

Positive Affirmation:_____
_____
_____

Thursday

Friday

Saturday

Notes

Week Of: _____

Sunday

_____ _____
_____ _____
_____ _____
_____ _____
_____ _____

Monday

_____ _____
_____ _____
_____ _____
_____ _____
_____ _____

Tuesday

_____ _____
_____ _____
_____ _____
_____ _____
_____ _____

Wednesday

_____ _____
_____ _____
_____ _____
_____ _____

Positive Affirmation:_____
_____
_____

Thursday

_____   _____
_____   _____
_____   _____
_____   _____

Friday

_____   _____
_____   _____
_____   _____
_____   _____

Saturday

_____   _____
_____   _____
_____   _____
_____   _____

Notes

_____   _____
_____   _____
_____   _____
_____   _____

Week Of: _____

Sunday
_____   _____
_____   _____
_____   _____
_____   _____
_____   _____

Monday
_____   _____
_____   _____
_____   _____
_____   _____
_____

Tuesday
_____   _____
_____   _____
_____   _____
_____   _____
_____

Wednesday
_____   _____
_____   _____
_____   _____
_____   _____

Positive Affirmation:_____
_____
_____

Thursday
_____   _____
_____   _____
_____   _____
_____   _____
_____   _____

Friday
_____   _____
_____   _____
_____   _____
_____   _____
_____   _____

Saturday
_____   _____
_____   _____
_____   _____
_____   _____
_____   _____

Notes
_____   _____
_____   _____
_____   _____
_____   _____

Tune your ears to wisdom, and concentrate on understanding.

Proverbs 2:2

May

SU	MO	TU	WE	TH	FR	SA
			1	2	3	4
5	6	7	8	9	10	11
12	13	14	15	16	17	18
19	20	21	22	23	24	25
26	27	28	29	30	31	

Notes:

_____
_____
_____
_____
_____
_____
_____
_____

Week Of: _____

Sunday

_____ _____
_____ _____
_____ _____
_____ _____
_____ _____

Monday

_____ _____
_____ _____
_____ _____
_____ _____
_____ _____

Tuesday

_____ _____
_____ _____
_____ _____
_____ _____
_____ _____

Wednesday

_____ _____
_____ _____
_____ _____
_____ _____
_____ _____

Positive Affirmation:_____
_____
_____

Thursday

_____   _____
_____   _____
_____   _____
_____   _____
_____   _____

Friday

_____   _____
_____   _____
_____   _____
_____   _____
_____   _____

Saturday

_____   _____
_____   _____
_____   _____
_____   _____
_____   _____

Notes

_____   _____
_____   _____
_____   _____
_____   _____

Week Of: _____

Sunday
_____ _____
_____ _____
_____ _____
_____ _____
_____ _____

Monday
_____ _____
_____ _____
_____ _____
_____ _____
_____ _____

Tuesday
_____ _____
_____ _____
_____ _____
_____ _____
_____ _____

Wednesday
_____ _____
_____ _____
_____ _____
_____ _____
_____ _____

Positive Affirmation:_____
_____
_____

Thursday

Friday

Saturday

Notes

Week Of: _____

Sunday

_____ _____
_____ _____
_____ _____
_____ _____
_____ _____

Monday

_____ _____
_____ _____
_____ _____
_____ _____
_____ _____

Tuesday

_____ _____
_____ _____
_____ _____
_____ _____
_____ _____

Wednesday

_____ _____
_____ _____
_____ _____
_____ _____
_____ _____

Positive Affirmation:_____
_____
_____

Thursday

Friday

Saturday

Notes

Week Of: _____

Sunday

——————————————— ———————————————
——————————————— ———————————————
——————————————— ———————————————
——————————————— ———————————————
——————————————— ———————————————

Monday

——————————————— ———————————————
——————————————— ———————————————
——————————————— ———————————————
——————————————— ———————————————
———————————————

Tuesday

——————————————— ———————————————
——————————————— ———————————————
——————————————— ———————————————
——————————————— ———————————————
———————————————

Wednesday

——————————————— ———————————————
——————————————— ———————————————
——————————————— ———————————————
——————————————— ———————————————

Positive Affirmation:_____
_____
_____

Thursday

Friday

Saturday

Notes

Work hard so you can present yourself to God and receive His approval. Be a good worker, one who does not need to be ashamed and who correctly explains the word of truth. *2 Timothy 2:15*

June

SU	MO	TU	WE	TH	FR	SA
						1
2	3	4	5	6	7	8
9	10	11	12	13	14	15
16	17	18	19	20	21	22
23	24	25	26	27	28	29
30						

Notes:

_____

_____

_____

_____

_____

Week Of: _____

Sunday

_____   _____
_____   _____
_____   _____
_____   _____
_____   _____

Monday

_____   _____
_____   _____
_____   _____
_____   _____
_____   _____

Tuesday

_____   _____
_____   _____
_____   _____
_____   _____
_____   _____

Wednesday

_____   _____
_____   _____
_____   _____
_____   _____
_____   _____

Positive Affirmation:_____
_____
_____

Thursday

_____   _____
_____   _____
_____   _____
_____   _____
_____   _____

Friday

_____   _____
_____   _____
_____   _____
_____   _____
_____   _____

Saturday

_____   _____
_____   _____
_____   _____
_____   _____
_____   _____

Notes

_____   _____
_____   _____
_____   _____
_____   _____

Week Of: _____

Sunday

_____   _____
_____   _____
_____   _____
_____   _____
_____   _____

Monday

_____   _____
_____   _____
_____   _____
_____   _____
_____   _____

Tuesday

_____   _____
_____   _____
_____   _____
_____   _____
_____   _____

Wednesday

_____   _____
_____   _____
_____   _____
_____   _____
_____   _____

Positive Affirmation:_____

_____

_____

Thursday

_____   _____
_____   _____
_____   _____
_____   _____
_____   _____

Friday

_____   _____
_____   _____
_____   _____
_____   _____
_____   _____

Saturday

_____   _____
_____   _____
_____   _____
_____   _____
_____   _____

Notes

_____   _____
_____   _____
_____   _____
_____   _____
_____   _____

Week Of: _____

Sunday

_____   _____
_____   _____
_____   _____
_____   _____
_____

Monday

_____   _____
_____   _____
_____   _____
_____   _____
_____

Tuesday

_____   _____
_____   _____
_____   _____
_____   _____
_____

Wednesday

_____   _____
_____   _____
_____   _____
_____   _____
_____

Positive Affirmation: _____
_____
_____

Thursday

_____   _____
_____   _____
_____   _____
_____   _____
_____   _____

Friday

_____   _____
_____   _____
_____   _____
_____   _____
_____   _____

Saturday

_____   _____
_____   _____
_____   _____
_____   _____
_____   _____

Notes

_____   _____
_____   _____
_____   _____
_____   _____

Week Of: _____

Sunday
_____ _____
_____ _____
_____ _____
_____ _____
_____

Monday
_____ _____
_____
_____ _____
_____ _____
_____ _____

Tuesday
_____ _____
_____ _____
_____ _____
_____ _____
_____ _____

Wednesday
_____ _____
_____
_____ _____
_____
_____ _____

Positive Affirmation:_____

_____

_____

Thursday

Friday

Saturday

Notes

The Lord of Heaven's Armies is a wonderful teacher, and He gives the farmer great wisdom.
Isaiah 28:28

July

SU	MO	TU	WE	TH	FR	SA
	1	2	3	4	5	6
7	8	9	10	11	12	13
14	15	16	17	18	19	20
21	22	23	24	25	26	27
28	29	30	31			

Notes:

_____
_____
_____
_____
_____
_____
_____
_____

Week Of: _____

Sunday

_____ _____
_____ _____
_____ _____
_____ _____
_____ _____

Monday

_____ _____
_____ _____
_____ _____
_____ _____
_____ _____

Tuesday

_____ _____
_____ _____
_____ _____
_____ _____
_____ _____

Wednesday

_____ _____
_____ _____
_____ _____
_____ _____

Positive Affirmation:_____
_____
_____

Thursday

Friday

Saturday

Notes

Week Of: _____

Sunday

_____ _____
_____ _____
_____ _____
_____ _____
_____ _____

Monday

_____ _____
_____ _____
_____ _____
_____ _____
_____ _____

Tuesday

_____ _____
_____ _____
_____ _____
_____ _____
_____ _____

Wednesday

_____ _____
_____ _____
_____ _____
_____ _____
_____ _____

Positive Affirmation:_____
_____
_____

Thursday

Friday

Saturday

Notes

Week Of: _____

Sunday

_____   _____
_____   _____
_____   _____
_____   _____
_____   _____

Monday

_____   _____
_____   _____
_____   _____
_____   _____
_____   _____

Tuesday

_____   _____
_____   _____
_____   _____
_____   _____
_____   _____

Wednesday

_____   _____
_____   _____
_____   _____
_____   _____
_____   _____

Positive Affirmation:_____
_____
_____

Thursday

_____   _____
_____   _____
_____   _____
_____   _____
_____   _____

Friday

_____   _____
_____   _____
_____   _____
_____   _____
_____   _____

Saturday

_____   _____
_____   _____
_____   _____
_____   _____
_____   _____

Notes

_____   _____
_____   _____
_____   _____
_____   _____

Week Of: _____

Sunday

_____ _____
_____ _____
_____ _____
_____ _____
_____ _____

Monday

_____ _____
_____ _____
_____ _____
_____ _____
_____ _____

Tuesday

_____ _____
_____ _____
_____ _____
_____ _____
_____ _____

Wednesday

_____ _____
_____ _____
_____ _____
_____ _____
_____ _____

Positive Affirmation:_____

_____

_____

Thursday

Friday

Saturday

Notes

Classmates & Friends

NAME	EMAIL	PHONE	BIRTHDAY

Classmates & Friends

NAME	EMAIL	PHONE	BIRTHDAY

NOTES

NOTES

NOTES